Go Chase It

The American Dream—It's Still Possible.

You Can Do It

By

Harsh Dharwad

To everybody with hopes and dreams of making it—to all the new graduates; first-time graduates in their families, who are dreaming big; and new immigrants and soon-to-be immigrants, who are wondering if it's still possible to "make it" in the United States.

And to my kids, who are still young and thinking about what they want to do with their lives.

For any enquiries please contact –

book.gochaseit@gmail.com

Table of Contents

Foreword 5

Preface 7

Part 1: HUMBLE BEGINNINGS 9

    A Second Chance 9

    Early Life 13

    My Greatest Advocate 16

    Low Aim Is a Crime 20

    Risking It All 25

    Applying for Schools 28

    Finding the Funds 33

    Believing in Success 36

    Humble Beginnings 40

    Hard Work Trumps Talent 44

    Persistence Pays Off 48

Part 2: NO SHORTCUTS 51

    The Smiths, American Football, and Thanksgiving 51

    Maximizing Strengths 54

    Running Out of Money 57

    The Goodness of People 60

    The Importance of Keeping in Touch 64

    And Networking! 67

    It's Not How Much Money You Make but How Much You Keep That Makes You Wealthy 70

    A Risk Worth Taking 73

Part 3: THE BIG LEAP TO SUCCESS 76

    The Importance of Preparing 76

Flying Business Class 79

Digging In 82

Take Bigger Risks Earlier in Life 87

Coming Home 90

Building Trust 94

Becoming CEO 97

Conclusion 99

About the Author 101

Foreword

By
Neda Moayedi

Educator | Leadership and Career Coach | Mindfulness Teacher

It is with great pleasure and excitement that I introduce you to Harsh Dharwad's book, Go Chase It. Within these pages, you'll embark on a journey—a path illuminated by hope, perseverance, and the unwavering belief in the American dream.

In today's world, where uncertainty often looms large and obstacles seem insurmountable, Harsh offers a beacon of inspiration. Through his own remarkable story and the timeless wisdom, he imparts, he demonstrates that the American dream is not merely a relic of the past but a living, breathing reality for those who dare to chase it.

Trusting the process, understanding the importance of mentors, and having someone who believes in you - ultimately leading to self-belief – Harsh emphasizes that natural talent alone isn't sufficient. Hard work and persistence are essential keys to success. With authenticity and clarity, he draws from personal experiences and the invaluable lessons learned along the way to highlight these fundamental truths.

As you turn these pages, you'll accompany Harsh on his personal odyssey—a journey marked by
triumphs and tribulations, setbacks, and successes. Through his candid reflections and heartfelt
anecdotes, you'll gain invaluable insights into the power of resilience, resourcefulness, and relentless determination.

Self-reflection and discovery are necessary to maximizing your strengths, Harsh reminds us, as he shares his own journey of introspection and growth. The importance of building relationships and staying in touch is also underscored, highlighting the transformative impact of genuine connections and community support.

Harsh's story resonates deeply with me, as I too have navigated the winding path of pursuing dreams in the face of adversity. His unfaltering belief in the possibility of a brighter tomorrow is contagious, reminding us all that no dream is too big and no challenge too daunting.

For the new graduates stepping out into the world with hope in their hearts, for the first-time
graduates in their families breaking barriers and forging new paths, and for the new immigrants and soon-to-be immigrants seeking opportunity and fulfillment, this book serves as a guiding light.

Through Go Chase It, Harsh invites you to dare to dream—to dream boldly, to dream fearlessly, and to pursue those dreams with unwavering passion and perseverance. In his words, you'll find not just a roadmap to success, but a testament to the enduring spirit of possibility that defines the American experience.

So, I invite you to embark on this transformative endeavor with an open heart and a steadfast resolve. As you immerse yourself in Harsh's story, may you find inspiration, guidance, and the resolute belief that yes, the American dream is still possible—and you can be the one to make it a reality.

Enjoy the chase!

Preface

I am not the most successful guy in this world—far from it. I did not set the world on fire, but I believe I achieved what I set out to achieve as a young kid, born into humble beginnings. Growing up in a small rural village overseas, the people around me were simple and hardworking, mostly doing manual labor. I struggled to find a role model. When I was in college, when I was starting my work career, I would've loved to have read a book like this or heard from somebody who'd been in my shoes and who'd gone through "the system," i.e., someone who'd traveled the pathway to success in corporate America. Since I am an immigrant to this wonderful country, I now call *home*, it's my intention that this book not only be a guide for those starting out their careers, but also new immigrants who are enrolled in college programs in the US as well as soon-to-be immigrants who would like to come to the US to study or start a new career here. It is my intention to ensure you are asking the right questions and focusing on the right areas to tap into your true potential.

Part 1: HUMBLE BEGINNINGS

A Second Chance

This is your second chance in life, and you can't screw it up.

Sometimes in life, we come upon a crossroads marked with multiple choices, where our decision is so instrumental to our future that the path we choose will irreversibly impact the trajectory of our lives. The decision to come to the United States was this big crossroads decision for me. I could either live a simple life with my family in India, or I could venture out to the unknown and try something completely different. With little means, I took the plunge. Perhaps it was a little naïve, but my immaturity was an asset in these situations because I was so focused on the reward that I didn't consider the risks, diving in head-first. I picked the path marked "USA" and thought, *This is what I'm doing.*

When I boarded that flight to America, I thought, *You can't screw this up, Harsh. Everybody in your family has backed you.* The only asset my dad ever owned was the house, and he put all his money into it and was very proud of it. My dad re-mortgaged the house to pay for my tuition. And my uncle coached me through the entire process of applying for schools and coming to the United States. I'd already graduated with a Bachelor's Degree in Engineering in my home country, and now I was applying for a master's program in the US. It really was an opportunity I didn't want to mess up. Not many people get a chance at a new life, so I felt the weightiness of my responsibility. I focused very much on this.

Before I left India, I had to figure out where to live and how to get around in the United States. *Where am I going to stay? Who is going to pick me up?* I emailed the International Student Association at Cleveland State University, who'd accepted me into their Master of Science program the previous summer. They offered to pick me up from the airport. They also offered me a place to stay with other students for ten days to give me time to figure everything out.

So I said goodbye to my family and hopped on that airplane where I told myself success was mandatory. This was my first time on an airplane. The plane flew from Bombay (Mumbai now) to Frankfurt, Germany, then to Cincinnati, Ohio, and last, to Cleveland. I was sandwiched in the middle seat in the very back row, but I didn't care. I was too excited.

When the plane landed, I told myself the most important thing, which I still remember: *Harsh, God has given you a second chance in life, and you've got to make everything out of it. It's all on you, and you have to grab it with both hands.*

I knew I was lucky to be here, in the US. This was a story I couldn't script. My uncle had helped; my father had helped, and it seemed like the stars had aligned. I got here with the blessing and influence of so many people. I knew I had to stay focused now. When you are that focused, it seems all fear goes out the window.

I stepped off the plane and looked around, followed the sign to baggage claim, picked up my enormous bags, and scanned the crowd. It was the pre-cell phone era, and I didn't know who'd be picking me up. A guy approached me and said, "Harsh?" It was a man from the International Student Association, there to drive me to the student apartment. I later asked him how he knew it was me.

"You just had *that look*." I must have looked quite lost. We drove forty minutes to downtown Cleveland where he dropped me off at an apartment with my two big bags containing all of my belongings.

When I walked inside, there were already three students there. It was a two-bedroom apartment, and we were waiting for two more international students to arrive. I was assigned to the couch. Had I been a little later, I might have had to settle for the floor.

I had planned to stay ten days; it turned into a month.

Early Life

I grew up in a tiny rural village in southern India. Many people around me had jobs in farming and agriculture, which was hard work in the hot sun. They didn't have fancy John Deere tractors or machines to do the work for them but relied on manual labor. They worked in rain, hail, or sunshine and began their days early—before the sun came up—and finished long after the sun disappeared. Despite all their hard work, the farmers remained poor. Sometimes the crops would fail. When they had a good harvest, they'd transport their crops to market in bullock carts along the rural roads. They had little support from the government; however, since achieving independence in 1947, the government has made more effort to provide infrastructure to villages. But when I was a child, it was still very much lacking in most places.

In India, there was a big problem with farmer suicides. I knew I wanted more from life for myself. At times, I felt like I did not belong because my dreams were much bigger than what others accepted.

There's nothing wrong with having a simple life. I was repeatedly told by friends to settle for what was in front of me. There was nothing wrong with the jobs available in my village—in my mind, they were no less important or less fulfilling careers, but I wanted more. In addition to my dad's guidance, I also had the advice of my grandfather, who would often say, "Don't be afraid to dream; you can do whatever you want, and you should set your mind to it and do it." That all sounded great, but everywhere I looked, people were simple and most were content with what they were doing.

My environment was the biggest hurdle to overcome to reach my dreams of a bigger life. At that time, if I had told my friends that I planned to go to the United States to become a CEO, everybody would have laughed at me and said, "Are you kidding?"

Out of all my friends and classmates, I had the biggest dream of them all, and in that sense, I was a little "out there." Because of this, I used to struggle with myself. And it was a constant battle.

First, I was young, so my thoughts were not clearly formulated. Second, I was not as mature as others my age, so I was caught in an internal battle where half of me thought, *I want to try something, and this is the time to do it*, and the other half of me argued, *I'm not sure if it's going to work out, and besides, this is probably the life I'm meant to live, so I should just stay here and do this.*

Luckily, I had one family member in particular who helped me resolve the internal debate.

My Greatest Advocate

The person who had the biggest impact on making my dreams a reality lived thirty hours away by train. He probably lived the farthest from where everybody else in my family lived. He was my uncle, and he was different too. He didn't have a job like the people in my village, so he never told me to settle. He was the only person I knew who wasn't working for somebody; he was his own boss. Aside from my uncle, I hadn't seen any real-life entrepreneurs. I'd only seen these types of people on television.

My uncle was the first person I'd known who'd done something different and on his own. He was a chemical engineer by trade and owned his own consulting company. My uncle was my mom's eldest brother and was always full of life. He had this immense energy—a charisma—that drew people to him.

Once in a while, he would visit us for family events or to see my grandfather, and I always looked forward to having conversations with him. I remember being very curious, listening closely to anything he had to say. He was also one of the few individuals I'd known who'd done a bit of traveling around the world, so I was always eager to hear him share his experiences.

Since I was still a little boy from a small town and had never before been on an airplane or left my country, I was keen to hear about different cultures, different infrastructure, and different foods from around the world. One day, he'd just returned from Europe, and he told me they had paved roads that went all the way up to the curb and a paved area to walk on called a *sidewalk*.

"Why do they have these?" I asked.

"It doesn't throw up a dust ball every time there's a little bit of wind," he explained.

In the villages, we had dirt roads, and aside from the dust, there was a lot of mud when it rained. In the city, there were paved roads, but they were paved for just the cars; there were no sidewalks or curbs. I thought this idea of paved curbs and sidewalks was brilliant, and I wanted to see them. He explained other oddities from around the world, too, such as cities where they planted trees to make the area look more aesthetically pleasing.

My uncle's ideas were different from most other adults I knew. I can remember one conversation about Colgate toothpaste. "Why do you think everybody uses it?" he asked.

I didn't know.

He said, "The company did an enormous amount of research on flavor profiles, got the sweetness just right, and then they marketed it brilliantly. This is why almost the entire world uses one brand of toothpaste when there are many to choose from." This was revolutionary for me.

At one family event, when all my cousins were around, he took me aside and said, "Whatever you do, you have to be very good at it." That stuck with me.

To figure out what I needed to do to apply for schools in the US and to prepare for entrance exams, I went to live with my uncle, and that is when I gained more profound insight into his life. My uncle consulted for various pharmaceutical companies, and he had his own office where people worked for him. He was an entrepreneur, and this was a unique concept to me. Although his business was not doing as well as he wanted, seeing someone in real life—as opposed to in books or on television—who was living this way helped me believe, *Hey, if he can do it, I think maybe it's possible for me to do something like that too.*

My uncle, for whatever reason, took an interest in me. I was bright, but I never had the best grades because I never tried all that hard. I didn't care much. To be honest, I would've much rather been playing cricket or other sports. But, as it turned out, I wasn't amazing enough at that to make a career out of it.

My uncle wasn't the only family member mentoring me; my grandparents were influential in a much different way and shaped the way I thought about the world and my place in it.

Low Aim Is a Crime

"Never aim low. Know that you can achieve whatever you want in life," said my grandfather. His words echoed through my mind as I lay in my childhood bed in our small town in India. It was 1998, and I was twenty-one years old. I was in college, studying to earn my undergrad degree in India, and bedridden, running a temperature of 104 degrees Fahrenheit. The fever wouldn't break. I'd lost a third of my body weight and was so weak, I could barely make it to the bathroom by myself. I was sweating rivers. My dad, who is a doctor, ordered my mom to keep me in bed. So that's where I spent what seemed like a very long two months. The pain was unlike anything I'd ever felt before or since. Typhoid can cause internal bleeding, and although not surviving the fever is rare, there was a moment when I felt so weak that I feared it might take me. I couldn't help but think, *Is this all I will accomplish with my life?*

One month earlier, when I'd first contracted the disease, I'd been careless. I had tried to rest and heal; my father had prescribed a healing regime of antibiotics, rest, and fluids, and it was working.

However, I was immature and impatient, and before I had fully recovered, I returned to school to finish a project. It turned out to be a terrible mistake.

In India, the journey to school was not easy. We lived about two hours from my school. To get to school, I had to take three buses. The first I boarded near my house, and it ran very unreliably—sometimes not coming at all. Usually, I abandoned the plan of taking the first bus. The other options were to take a "tuk-tuk," which cost $1—more than I could afford—or walk. Nine times out of ten, I chose to walk the three miles to the next bus stop, along dusty roads and in the heat. That decision after my initial illness put me back in the bed.

I was now sicker than before. All I could do was fall in and out of a feverish sleep. I spent months staring at the ceiling and wrestling with stomach cramps and headaches. I'd stumble to the bathroom down the hall, which, in my weak state, felt miles away, as though I had hiked a mountain. It was torture, and the worst part was there was nothing I could do to get better faster. I had to let go of control and trust the healing process. But it was taking a long time, and I didn't feel like I was making much progress.

At my lowest and probably most dramatic point, I told my mom, "I might die. This might be what takes me." This obviously scared her, and she and my dad talked. Then another doctor was called in for a second opinion.

The second doctor arrived and examined me, and I could tell by the look in his eyes that he knew my condition was deteriorating; I was severely dehydrated. He gave me a new healing regimen involving intravenous fluids and medication, and after another rough month, I was finally recovering. Again, my fever eased, and I could leave the house.

This time, I promised myself I'd take it slowly. However, it wasn't easy. I had lost an incredible amount of weight, and I hadn't had much to begin with. Typhoid is transferred through contaminated water or food washed in contaminated water, and I was still paranoid about everything I ate. I was also scared of overexerting myself because I didn't want to return to a bedridden state. Even though I was up and about, mentally, I was still in a very low place. I was full of fear, jobless, and clueless, with no idea which direction to take in my life. Out of desperation, I worked a mindless job at the university, making $27 a month. I was so disappointed in myself. I wanted a bigger life, and I knew I was better than this.

Up to this point, I hadn't been taking life seriously. I was lax with my studies, only just passing my exams. I had no direction, but I still had big dreams. Aside from dreams of becoming a famous cricketer—which was, by this stage, fairly lofty—I had no real plan for what I would do with my life.

My grandfather repeated these words to me many times, and they hit home in a way they never had before: "Never aim low; low aim is a crime." Because of him, I grew up thinking I could be whatever I wanted and that I could, and *would*, make something of myself.

Yet, there I was, nearly graduated and barely alive. During what was supposed to be the peak of my life, I had fallen gravely ill.

It was at this time that my uncle intervened and suggested I should go to the United States to study. But when he said this to my parents and me, we thought he was joking. I was feeling a bit lost, and the thought of going to another country had never crossed my mind. I was afraid I'd be more lost. But I knew I wanted to do more with my life, so I risked thinking about what my life in the US might look like. I was afraid because I didn't know how the world worked outside of my village. And if I did go to the US, what would my life really look like?

But with the encouragement from my grandfather and the picture of success I had from my uncle, I thought there was some hope. So I kept dreaming. Then one day, my dreaming turned into a decision.

Risking It All

No one in our family—and, for that matter, no one we knew—had ever relocated abroad. It was unheard of. In India, people exist in nuclear and extended family systems. It is common for three generations to live in the same home. In the West, we value "individualism"; however, in India, we have a "community-style" society, which values interdependence and cooperation and the family as the nucleus of this structure. To leave one's family could be seen as abandoning your duty to care for them. I was lucky in that my grandfather and uncle, and eventually my father, supported my decision to leave. My uncle said, "I know for a fact that you can do this." He advocated for me in a way I couldn't because he saw the implications of me not doing it and was able to articulate this to my dad in a way my dad accepted. He pointed me in a direction I had not thought of (coming to the US), and thus changed the course of my life.

Once I decided I was going to America, my family decided it would be best for me to live with my uncle because he could best help prepare me for the trip by taking me through the process of applying to schools, preparing me for the tests, selecting the best schools to which to apply, and introducing me to his friend, who could tutor me for the English test. I boarded a train for the twenty-five-hour journey, which was the first time I'd traveled that far on my own, and it felt like a big adventure. This was the first time I experienced life outside my bubble.

My uncle lived in Indore. Just being that far away gave me a new perspective on life. I stayed with my uncle for twelve months, and the experiences I had there shattered my old belief system. How I saw the world completely changed. For one, it was the first time I felt I was treated as an *individual*. My uncle, someone whom I had so much respect for, spoke to me like an adult. He asked for my feedback, debated with me, challenged my beliefs, and talked to me about all sorts of topics, ranging from money to girls. He taught me how to be charismatic and how to hold a conversation, and emphasized the importance of both in being successful.

I also received the invaluable experience of seeing him in action. Unlike anyone else in my family, he owned something. He was the boss; he didn't work for anybody else. As I mentioned before, this was something I'd only ever seen on television. Until then, it wasn't reality. I had a new realization: here is someone *doing it. And if he can do it here in India, I can do it even better in the US.*

Applying for Schools

It was time to start the process of getting to the United States. It wasn't an easy one. My uncle's friends had experience with this process, which included preparing for the English language test; choosing the best five schools to apply to (applying to any more would incur an additional cost); and filling out the college application forms. The list of the to-dos also included completing tons of paperwork, applying for a passport, and studying for academic exams.

Up first was the GRE, a graduate-level exam. I already had the math skills to do well, but my English skills were novice, to say the least. This test was tough for native English speakers! I wondered how I'd fare.

Growing up, we only spoke Kannada at home and school. In eighth grade, I was sent to live with my grandfather to attend English school. Half the time, I had no clue what the teacher was saying, but this is how I learned English. So it was safe to say the GRE would be an uphill battle. I was lucky that my uncle's friend volunteered to be my personal English coach. She invited me into her home and gave me vocabulary tests. Still, every time I glanced at the practice exam, I didn't know half the words. However, after some time and a lot of practice, I was ready for the test. I took it and did reasonably well. I have such gratitude for this woman, Swathi Jain, and her selfless generosity.

Next on the list was the passport. I applied for the passport months ago and received nothing, no notifications or next steps. It felt as if it was taking a lifetime—one thing India and the US have in common! I had finally decided that I needed to go to the passport office, which was a thirty-hour bus ride to Bangalore. It was the most awful bus ride of my life. The bus driver was reckless, and the other drivers we passed were equally chaotic; it was as if they all had death wishes. The roads were horrible, and that's an understatement; there were so many potholes that, to this day, I still have lower back pain from an injury I sustained on that bus ride. And the worst part was that I had to visit this passport office not once, but *three times*. Eventually, after another four months, my passport arrived.

With the GRE and the passport out of the way, I was ready to apply to schools. I had spent my entire life in India, so I was lost regarding this step. *To which colleges should I apply?* I knew nothing. Nothing about the schools. Nothing about the geography. Nothing about the weather. The *U.S. News & World Report* ranks US universities, so I started there. I picked up a copy from a library. I decided to apply to the schools that had little to no application fees. That's how I made my decision. So with the help of the *U.S. News & World Report* and my uncle's friend's US credit card, I sent off my applications to five schools, all on the East Coast. I was accepted to three.

The last and final step was the US Visa process. Similar to getting a passport, getting a visa was a mess. My father and I took a train to the US Embassy in Bombay, now called Mumbai. There was no opportunity to make an appointment, so my father and I got up at two in the morning and readied ourselves to wait outside in line all day long.

After waiting six hours, I was called, given a token, and stepped inside the US Embassy. My father waited for me outside. During this time, there were no cell phones and definitely no smartphones. He waited for me the entire time I was inside, which ended up being around four hours. I can't say enough about how much I appreciated him joining me on the journey. This was really the first time he and I went somewhere together, just the two of us. During this pivotal moment in my life, he took the time out of his busy schedule to support me. It meant a lot.

Inside the embassy, everything was in complete disarray. It was crowded and loud, and I couldn't hear most of the announcements over the loudspeaker. When I did hear the occasional announcement, a lot of them were in a language I didn't speak or recognize (Gujarati). I had to wait patiently for announcements in English, and I felt like I might have missed an announcement about me. For two hours, I sat with my little token and watched person after person get called. And I got nervous. I thought about my family's financial situation and whether that could affect my visa approval. I thought about all those stories I had heard about strict interviewers who denied everybody. *Would they deny me?*

At last, my token number was called. The attendant at the window explained to me that my application had been pre-approved. All my worrying had been for nothing. There were no problems with my financial situation. No interview was necessary. I could come by that evening and pick up my visa. My last step to get to the US was complete.

Finding the Funds

Out of my letters of acceptance, I selected Cleveland State University in Ohio. My uncle's friend told me it was a decent university with small classes in which I could maximize my learning.

Now the real question had to be addressed: *How am I going to pay for this?* I approached my father, who had doubts about this whole thing from the start. My parents were always cautious people and were especially careful with their expenses. So when I asked if they could fund my going to the United States, my father told me, "This may be too much of a risk. Why don't you focus on doing something here? It will be too expensive. Just do what you're doing. Why bother going to the United States? We don't have the means, so we can't afford for you to go."

This came as a shock to me since he'd been supportive in recent months. Now, when it was time to fund the venture, he thought there was too much risk. Too many unknowns. I was disappointed. I had invested so much in this, and it had taken a lot of time and effort to get where I was. And although I had always had a feeling it might not be possible, I had been finally believing in the dream. If I was honest with myself, I really wanted it.

Then my uncle stepped in. He advocated for me when I didn't know how to advocate for myself. To this day, I don't know why he did it; he just did. He said *no* to my father's *no*. He called my parents and told them, "He has spent too much time going down this path. What are you worried about? He has done the hard work. At least let him try." He knew this was the only way our family could advance in the world. He knew someone would have to take this risk at some point. Why shouldn't it be me? Not sending me was not an option in his eyes. Thanks to his charisma, powerful argument, and persistence—and a helpful word from my grandfather—my parents eventually gave in. I hope one day I can do something similar for someone else in my life.

I thought I'd be overjoyed by my dad's eventual support, but I was scared. While I was trying to decide on the school, I went through a lot of internal debate. I asked myself, "Money aside, do I even have the tools to succeed? Do I have the acumen, the intelligence, the personality required to make it or not? Should I try this or not? Should I stick with what I'm doing, or can I do better than this?" I had to fight through the inner turmoil. That was the biggest obstacle. Once I made up my mind, I developed a laser-like focus.

Once my father agreed to help financially, we still needed to find the funds. My parents and I went to the bank to look into getting a loan. To get the loan, my father would have to use our house as collateral. He agreed to do it. My father didn't just buy this house. He *built* this house, and he'd spent his life working hard to pay it off. This house was something he was so proud of—a two-story, three-bedroom, single-family home with a small yard. It was also our only asset. It took a lot of courage for my father to do this for me.

The weight of the family's future was on my shoulders. There was no room to screw up. People had put their faith in me, and now it was my turn to deliver.

In return for the house, the bank loaned us nearly $8,000, enough to cover about a semester and a half of the university costs. The rest I had to figure out. But I was on my way!

Believing in Success

When I was twelve, my mother said, "The schools aren't very good here, and I think for you to do better in your life, you need to go to a different school and learn English. So I'm going to send you to live with your grandparents." She was referring to her parents.

I moved towns, transitioned into my grandparents' home, and started at the English school.

Don't aim low. Low aim is a crime.

You can do whatever you want in your life.

You just have to focus and be committed and work hard for it.

My grandfather said these things with such conviction that I believed him. The self-confidence I've gained in my abilities was developed because of my grandfather.

He was speaking from personal experience. As a teenager, my grandfather had run away from home. His family wanted him to drop out of school and work on the family farm, but he loved studying and wanted to remain in school. He left and built a life for himself;

he figured out life on his terms and that gave him a certain level of confidence. Then it must have rubbed off on me.

My grandmother was educated and spoke English, which was unusual for people of that age group. Her father, my great-grandfather, had worked for the British Government, and so he made sure his daughters learned English. He also introduced her to recreational activities, such as riding bicycles and playing music, which was unusual for girls at that time.

It was quite hard to start school in a new town, and most of the time, I didn't know what was going on since everything was taught in English. My grandmother helped me a lot because she would speak to me in English at night. And whenever my grandfather asked me to do something, he'd explain why, which was great because I was inquisitive. Even now, I ask a lot of questions because a task has to make sense to me. If it makes sense, I'm happy to do it.

Together, they became a gigantic knowledge bank for me. My grandparents were humble people, very hardworking, and never took shortcuts. They knew hard work paid. As a teenage boy, I was just beginning to understand the world, and living with them gave me a great worldview. My grandfather would sit and debate with me, and my grandmother could talk about nearly any topic. She was amazing—the sweetest person I've ever known, to this day.

My grandfather, who retired from a fairly senior position at the university, was well-read and charming. People would visit our home to say hello, and my grandfather would be the star of the show. I remember when he was in his eighties, everybody would stand around listening to him, mesmerized by him. He spoke in English and his mother tongue very well. I learned early on from him that talent and hard work are important, but equally important is presentation. All these elements played an integral part in my value system while growing up in their home, and they have helped me get to where I am today.

My belief in myself also came from collecting evidence of and recognizing my own capabilities. From early on, I was a fast learner; I picked things up quicker than most, and this made me realize, *I'm not bad. I can figure this out.*

I've always had an overwhelming feeling that I should do something with my life. I'd say to my friends, "I think I'm good. I don't know how I will succeed or what I will do, but I feel I have enough talent to do something great." As these words used to leave my mouth, I felt nervous I would become a laughingstock, one of those guys who talks a big game but has zero delivery. So for a while, I kept these ideas to myself because I didn't want to come across as boastful or over-confident.

But my grandparents would never let that happen. Their humility taught me how to view myself humbly and still harbor big dreams and self-confidence. My other grandparents (on my dad's side) were also humble, so I can only hope I got a double portion.

Humble Beginnings

My other grandfather (my dad's father) stood like a tower above me. He was so big, he could have played American football. As a gentle giant, he was also very patient and calm; I don't think I ever saw him get angry. My grandmother (my dad's mom), on the other hand, was the fire in their relationship. When she was upset with him, the entire house would know about it. Usually, he'd just sit and nod, and sometimes, very politely, he'd respond, "I'm your husband. Please talk nicely to me." He was so graceful, and he worked as a schoolteacher.

When I was ten or eleven, I remember him taking me for walks every day. We'd walk a mile to the main road and sit on a bench. We'd sit and watch the cars, birds, and trees for a while, then we'd go home. This was our evening routine.

We used to call ourselves middle-class, but really, we came from a humble background. When I was growing up, I don't remember ever going on vacation (at least, not what most people think of as vacations in the West). We did go out to eat once a month, so we weren't extremely poor either.

When you don't have a lot of money growing up, one of the drivers is to succeed and to succeed at all costs. I didn't take no for an answer; I hustled my way through and tried to figure out my way over hurdles as I went. Some people call it *grit*, and they say it's impossible to teach. I think they're right, but I had good role models.

My frugality and thoughtfulness about spending is still there. The difference between how I used to live—counting pennies—and how I spend now (e.g., new cars, weekends away with my son, and a fancy gym membership) is vast. That gulf is so big that it still makes me feel guilty sometimes. When I buy something nice, part of me feels like I shouldn't get it. It's a form of "Why me?" I watch myself to make sure I'm not splurging or spoiling my kids. It's hard to teach drive and hunger when you're not living in want, and the only way I've seen it develop is through adversity.

When I was eleven years old and still living at home with my parents, my aunt, my dad's sister, was suffering from breast cancer. She lived with us at the time, and my dad was helping out with her treatment, but the chemotherapy drugs were extremely expensive. And my dad was, at the same time, building our house.

One day, I had an upcoming field trip, and I really wanted to go. The total cost was going to be $3. My dad told me it wouldn't be the right use of their money, that it should go to helping my aunt's treatments. I was so disappointed that I missed out on that trip. As an adult, I completely understand it, but as a kid, I was devastated. I remember thinking at the end of that day, "Whatever happens in life, I have to work hard enough so that I don't find myself or my family in that position ever again."

These kinds of experiences—like being denied something I was excited about as a teenager—built my character and drive to succeed. If my kids want to go on a field trip, they should be able to go. Now, I can provide that for them. But it doesn't come without sacrifice. These experiences helped me build a value system whereby I don't take shortcuts; I trust the process, and I know it's going to be okay in the long run.

My dad used to tell me, "Whatever you become is on you. You're responsible for your own life. There are no handouts. Nothing is coming your way." I remember thinking that my dad didn't have a business that could provide me with a job. I knew that connections mattered, and I didn't have any. I knew I couldn't wait for handouts or for my dad or relatives to help me.

So I worked hard, and that made so much difference.

Hard Work Trumps Talent

My uncle had taught me through his examples of successful companies, like the maker of Colgate, about the drive toward excellence and that for someone to be good at something, they must really work at it. It doesn't come by luck or winning the lottery—well, rarely. When a product like a phone appears seamless and intuitive, it's not by accident. Somebody, likely many people, has spent a lot of time developing it, fine-tuning it.

My hunger, coupled with knowing I had to work hard, was where I knew success would come from.

Growing up, I wasn't the most successful kid. I knew I was intelligent, but I didn't have the best grades because I wasn't motivated to study. I was just a regular kid, and I wanted to play outside like most kids do. As a teenager living with my grandfather, I was introduced to his neighbor, a former professor who loved books. He opened a part of his house as a library and the townspeople came to read his books; it was a very generous gesture for him to welcome anybody who wanted to read. A few of my friends and I would visit and sit there and read. It was all very professional—we'd have to sign in and log which book we were reading. Some of the professor's collection was expensive and hard to find. This was part of the attraction of visiting and why many people went (and why we had to sign in!).

A few of my friends were excellent students with good grades, and the teachers knew them well. I would tag along and spend a couple of hours after school reading with them. And because it was my neighbor's house, it was also convenient.

One day, my mom was speaking with the professor, and she was complaining about me, telling him I wasn't as focused as the other kids. I overheard the professor say, "He is a late bloomer in life. I see talent. I don't think you have to worry about him. Just hang with him and trust him." *This felt good to hear and made me believe in myself more. I realized I could succeed.*

As a kid, I was looking for optimism and a way to succeed. I inherently knew to trust the process and, at some point, I realized the way to get ahead in life was through education. It was important to study, but growing up, I wanted to be a sportsman (an *athlete*, as Americans call them). That was my dream, to play sports professionally. I was good, but I wasn't the best, nor did I have any formal coaching until rather late in my life. I think that hurt me. I could have been much better, but my family wasn't into sports. Whatever talent I had I played with, but I didn't have anyone to mentor or guide me.

When I was sixteen, I started noticing the boys on the playing field around me getting physically bigger and faster than me. I understood that the professional coaching they were receiving had helped them. I got my first professional coaching when I was sixteen. I really loved it; it was my ultimate dream, and I would have worked hard to do it. But I knew intuitively that being a professional athlete wasn't ever going to happen. Some of the kids who played better than me didn't have as much natural talent, but they were more disciplined and worked harder. They had a more structured approach. This realization—this truth—taught me something very valuable: even though someone may have natural talent, it wasn't sufficient in itself to succeed in life. Hard work is equally important, if not more important, than natural talent on the road to success.

These days, I take my son to soccer practice and have been doing so since he was in elementary school. He's getting professional coaching, which is much more common in the US. Maybe, one day, he'll have the opportunity to play professionally if that is something he wants to do. I've done my part; I've passed on the truth that hard work and persistence are key factors.

Persistence Pays Off

When I was in junior high, I was pretty relaxed and happy to get Bs on my report cards and then go do other things with my time. I had an arrogant attitude; I knew I was smart, and if I studied, I'd do well.

But one semester, I failed two classes. This was an eye-opener! I said to myself, *Obviously, you're not as smart as you thought.* I'd tried to cram a semester's worth of study into two days before the test. That was a painful lesson.

The positive side was that I realized I don't like to fail; I *want* to succeed.

When I applied for my first full-time job in India, I flipped through the newspaper. This was where employers used to advertise. I ran my finger down the columns of classifieds and paused when I read an ad that said the employer would reimburse candidates' travel to the interview. So I bought a bus ticket, traveled to the interview, and met with the hiring manager, but I didn't get the job. I asked to be reimbursed for the bus travel, and they told me, "Out of all the people who came to interview, you're the only one who has asked to be reimbursed." There were some problems because they hadn't been asked by any other applicants for reimbursement before because it was such a nominal amount of money. I had finished my interview in the morning and then had to wait until 4 p.m. to get the money for the bus. Eventually, they did reimburse me, but it took the entire day because they weren't prepared.

It was a very painful lesson for a young kid like me because I didn't have a lot of money. I was trying to get a job to make money, and I realized that it was not going to be easy. I realized that day that life is hard. I thought, *If you want to make something out of yourself, you can't take yourself lightly. You have to take yourself very seriously, and it's going to be hard work.*

I decided that nobody was coming with handouts and that, essentially, I was alone. In some ways, I had grown up sheltered by my parents and my family. I wish I'd taken my education more seriously early on. My friends had taken their studies seriously, and some of them had jobs and were working in different industries. That's when I thought, *I have to go back to the drawing board and take this seriously; I have to take action.* This reinforced what I knew to be true: things aren't going to come easy, and I have to put in the hard work.

Even though I already knew this, I needed a little kick in the backside to make it real.

Part 2: NO SHORTCUTS

The Smiths, American Football, and Thanksgiving

Once my plane touched down in the US, I felt I'd been dropped into a new culture—because I had. Multiple cultures, really. *Everything* was different. I was amazed. I have always had a curious nature, so I loved every minute of it. All I could do was grasp each difference and learn. There were so many simple things, especially mannerisms, I just didn't understand. Strangers said hello as they passed each other on the sidewalk, and this activity was completely foreign to me.

I made friends from America and from other corners of the globe. They were hugely helpful as they explained the nuances of their cultures to me. One day, they taught me all about American football, and after that, I was hooked. Still, today, watching football is one of my favorite hobbies.

During my first semester, I took up an opportunity to have a traditional Thanksgiving dinner with an American family. It was through a university program that matched hosts and students from other countries. I mean, *why not?* I'll never forget the family: the Smith family. Yes, they had the most common American last name. That day, they welcomed me into their home—a big, beautiful house surrounded by trees, like it was in a sort of jungle. It was something I had never experienced. I watched them all help prepare the meal, and I helped, too, but watching them work together was my favorite part. The food was tasty to them, but I found it quite bland. I even asked for hot sauce. They all laughed, of course, and I was given a jar of jalapenos.

But humor aside, I was grateful this family had opened their home to me, while I was a complete stranger to them, and they did it for an intimate family holiday. They gave me a special glimpse into American life, and I would never forget it.

These new moments, people, and experiences taught me to take the time to *learn*. Learn about the culture, the mannerisms, the sports, and the customs of other people and places. It's such a beautiful thing. Without it, I would've wasted so many incredible opportunities, and I wouldn't have learned so many of the passions, hobbies, and beliefs that I have today.

Maximizing Strengths

While I did soak up the culture and the social life of the United States, I was here to study and work hard. In class, I was focused. I put my best into everything I did, every assignment. I studied and worked. *Constantly*. This was *my* opportunity. I felt lucky just to be here. I found that the American university-style education system suited my learning style. Growing up in India, education was centered on perfection. It was all about producing *exactly* what your teacher wanted, and I could never do it quite right. But in the United States, there was an emphasis on exploration and discovering the *why* behind everything. Here, in this learning environment, I succeeded.

Aside from studying, there wasn't much for me to do. I had no television, no computer, no cell phone, and zero money. All my time was spent studying, working, or spending time alone. This was a big change for me. Back in India, I had always been surrounded by aunts, uncles, cousins, and friends. That wasn't always good, either.

I was constantly compared to my cousins, and there were expectations to meet. This placed a lot of pressure on me. But with my newfound "alone time," I came to realize that many of the views I had about myself were views that others had put on me. So, for the first time, I had the space for introspection. Reflection. Even self-study.

This helped me discover what I'm good at, what I need to work on, and what I need to watch out for. I was beginning to understand the areas where I could excel and the areas where I needed help. That itself, I learned, is a valuable skill. In fact, it's the key to understanding the best way to succeed: maximize your strengths and let them shine. Don't let your weaknesses be your downfall. Manage them. Take math, for example. Some of us may struggle with it, while others will excel at it. This doesn't mean you need to change. You just need to be *aware* of which one you are.

I learned I was very good with people and could communicate effectively; I could interact with people from different backgrounds. Yes, I was an engineer, but I could relate just as easily to musicians as I could to other engineers. I was also good with strategy—I could figure out how to analyze things and create paths to solve problems, and I could break down complex problems into simple blocks to understand and execute.

On the other hand, I realized that I wasn't as good at letting go of problems I was stuck on; I'd keep digging into it and getting pulled into it and losing a lot of time on that one problem. Once I realized this, I learned to step away, put it to the side, and give it time to sit. Then I'd come back to it from a different perspective. I also had a problem with not being able to say no without burning bridges. I discovered a way to phrase things in a way that helped me protect my time and maintain relationships. Another area that I struggled with was finances. I didn't know how to think about finance or how to invest money or how to balance my checkbook. I decided to take an interest in finance and educate myself, and this made a huge difference in my wealth management.

Running Out of Money

When I wasn't studying or spending time alone, I was working. The loan from my father covered one semester. It was on me to come up with the rest of the money to pay for the next semester, and the next. I had to get a job, and I had to get one that was part-time and on campus since I was an international student and there were restrictions on how many hours I could work. There was also the requirement that I work on campus.

Thankfully, I found a job. It was one that nobody else wanted. I was the new university parking attendant. I spent plenty of freezing cold Ohio mornings in a steel booth, alone, with no heater, no cell phone, and no source of entertainment. For my efforts, I made $5.50 per hour, which was the minimum wage in Ohio at the time. Even though it was a bit rough, I couldn't complain too much because I was making money.

After working for a year as a parking attendant, I was lucky enough to find a better job. Cleveland State had a program with one of the local school districts where they'd take high school students from underprivileged areas and offer them free tutoring with university students. They hired me as one of their tutors, so it became my job to help students with their math homework. This job was much more rewarding and much more inspiring.

Despite these two jobs, though, I was still coming up short for each semester's tuition.

Finals were done and the end of the semester was upon me, but despite my hard work, I still did not have enough money to pay for the next semester. I knew I couldn't ask my father for more money; he had sacrificed enough. I was stuck, and the odds were stacked against me. I was in a new country, people were different from those at home, and I didn't have a support system of family and friends here.

My best plan was to get a credit card and put my tuition on that.

In one of my classes, I was sitting with a group of students where everybody was sharing their plans for winter break. Our professor came up to us and casually asked where we were spending it. Some students were returning home; others were going on trips, but in a moment of honesty, I told the professor, "I'm going to work and try to figure out how I'm going to pay for next semester." The rules dictated that during winter break, which was about a month long because there was no school, I was allowed to work forty hours a week. I didn't feel bad about working; I was just being realistic.

When the class ended, the professor asked me to stay behind and tell him more about my situation. "Walk with me," he said.

"Sure," I replied.

And my circumstances changed again.

The Goodness of People

The professor led me to the dean's office. He introduced me to the dean of Electrical Engineering, saying, "Hash (Hirsch) doesn't know this, but he is the only student in my class getting an A. I would like to recommend him for a scholarship." It felt surreal because I was not expecting this at all. I had no idea this could be a possibility, and it would be a huge relief financially. I felt a ray of hope—suddenly having a reason to be optimistic that this could work out. The dean told him he would look into it and asked if there were any projects or work I could do. My professor confirmed there were.

As we walked back to the class, I thanked my professor profusely. I hadn't asked him to do that. I hadn't even asked for his help. He just offered it. He'd done it out of the goodness of his heart, and I am forever grateful for that.

Not quite three weeks later, I got a call from the dean's office. It was good news; I was approved to be a teacher's assistant! The department would pay my tuition, and I would work ten hours a week, helping my professor with his research. Two weeks later, I got a call from the assistant to the chair who asked me to come in and sign the paperwork. I dropped everything and practically ran there before they changed their mind.

This taught me that there are good people in this world. My professor didn't have any incentive to do anything for me. He did it out of the kindness of his heart. That tuition assistance not only paid for the next semester but for the rest of my education. It taught me that if I was honest and genuine and worked hard—if I gave everything my best effort—there would be people who would notice. I'd come across people willing to take a chance on me. I also learned not to be afraid to do the right thing and not to be a naysayer or doubter but to trust in life and the goodness of people.

Perhaps the biggest takeaway of all during that season was that America evaluates you for who you are, not where you are from. It didn't matter who my father was, or what my bank balance was, or that I was different. None of that was important for my success. What mattered was that I worked hard. And I was recognized for that. It showed me that, in the United States, anything is possible if you are willing to persevere and work smart. Of course, there were long periods of time where I didn't know where my next meal was coming from and long hours of hard work, but if you are hungry enough and want it, *here* you will be given the opportunity to succeed, or even just participate. Sure, I didn't get to have the typical college experience that many students have. I didn't get to go out every night or party like others did. I had to sacrifice some of my time. But in doing so, I found luck and success. After all, luck is not as random as people might think; it comes about when hard work meets opportunity.

———

My university experience was life-changing. I highly encourage others to immerse themselves in a new culture, one where there is greater opportunity found when they leave home the way I did.

At university, there were many international students. I had no idea there would be that many. This was both a good and a bad thing. It was a great opportunity for students from all over the world to get together and meet people from different cultures. But there were *so many* international students that it made it easy for some to stay in their comfort zones. They continued to speak their native languages, watched their usual television programs, and stayed in circles with people from their country of origin. In my opinion, they could've done all that in their own countries!

I had a different approach. I tried to go to as many school events and fairs as I could. I would be out and socialize any chance I had, not being afraid to meet people, to say *hello*, to branch out. My mission was to dive into American culture, food, and pastimes.

You know what happened? Everything, from the baseball games to weekend barbecues, made me fall in love with the United States. The university gave me an education in engineering, but my *experiences* in the United States gave me an education in life.

My only regret? I should've used the university gym more!

The Importance of Keeping in Touch

Before I graduated, I started the process of finding a job. A *real* job. It was 2001. The economy was awful—not as bad as it was several years later in 2008 and 2009 but still bad. I had no idea where to start. I didn't even know how to interview properly in this country. Every country does these things differently. I had to get started.

The first thing I did was attend a mock interview set up by the university's career services. It was a great opportunity to have conversations, meet professionals, and get pointers. I met someone who worked in the Human Resources department. I introduced myself, we talked, and I had a good time talking. I got his contact information and was *determined* to stay in touch with him. Now and then, I would just check in with him and say hi.

The second thing I did was ditch the online applications. They just weren't working. I kept thinking, *I just need to get in front of the person who makes decisions*. I learned that every county in the

United States has a chamber of commerce. And I learned each chamber of commerce sells a book that lists *every* business in that county. *Perfect. I'll start there.*

And I did. I started calling each company, asking if they were hiring. When I called one company, the owner, Jeff, picked up. I introduced myself, told him a bit about myself, and asked if he was hiring. He wasn't. But he was curious about me, and we had a lengthy conversation. I asked if I could come see his business, see how they did things. He said, "Sure."

I borrowed a suit, printed my resume, and headed over. Jeff met me in the reception area and showed me around the office. He kindly interviewed me, despite not having any available positions. Jeff also gave me some advice, and I asked him to call me if he ever needed help with anything. We kept in touch.

There's a fine line when it comes to keeping in touch with people who can bring you opportunities. If you pester them, they will ignore you. If you stay away for too long, they will forget you. Checking in now and then will ensure you stay in the back of their minds when openings or positions arrive.

One of the random times I followed up with the human resources fellow I met at the mock interview, he told me that his company had an internship role open. I went in and interviewed, but I didn't get it. I was sent the obligatory *sorry* message. But I still kept in touch with him, and eventually, he had another position open up.

This internship would be building an internal website for the company. I had done absolutely no web work, but I thought, *Why not interview anyway*? This time, they picked me. They picked me but not because I was the best candidate. In fact, they had other applicants who were more qualified than me. They picked me because they liked my background . . . and maybe my persistence. I went through the entire internship, and it was a great experience. I got to see how the healthcare industry operated, and I developed a website from scratch—again, something I hadn't done before. The website was finished fairly quickly, and I was given other assignments to work on for the remainder of my time. One of these assignments was to develop a proof of concept for various medical devices. I knew the day was coming when I'd need to find a paying full-time job; it was approaching fast. I was hopeful that this internship would turn into the full-time job I needed.

And Networking!

At the end of the internship, I was left without a job. There was one available in a different department, but I interviewed and didn't get it. I felt dejected and disappointed—I had made a lot of contributions during the internship, though. I'd completed at least three different projects successfully and felt as if I had done enough. This rejection made me feel gutted. Suddenly, I realized how much impact my immediate boss had on my getting a job or not. My boss was a very nice guy, but he wasn't really invested in my role. The intern who won the job had a boss who was completely engaged and invested in the internship and the intern, which meant he could more clearly articulate how good of a job his intern had done. His intern had, in fact, done a wonderful job. But I learned how impactful having a good boss is in your career progression.

So I networked. Before I left, I walked around the company, visiting other departments, asking if they needed any help or had any openings. I was not shy about it. The IT group said they had an opening for another internship, but they told me I was overqualified for it. I took it anyway. That internship came and went, and I asked again for a full-time position. There were none.

As a Plan B, I called Jeff, the owner of the first company I approached, whom I had met after cold-calling companies from the list I bought from the chamber of commerce. I asked him if he had any full-time work, and he told me he had a *little* job. I came in and interviewed for it. This interview was a breeze. I had known everyone in the room for a while because I had kept in touch. It was then I got my first full-time job.

Here's what I learned from this journey: never underestimate the value of networking. The only reason I won my internships and my first full-time job was because of the relationships I had built. Human interaction and connection go a long way. Further than I imagined. How many other applicants had kept in touch with this company for over a year? Probably none. Plus, in the US, I had no friends, family, or people to recommend me as a good worker, or even a good person. I had to make those connections myself.

It is important to take the time to network and stay in touch. When an opportunity comes up, they will think of you if you are a decent person with a decent amount of talent.

Although I was grateful for my first job, it wasn't all that I desired. When Jeff had said, "little," he'd meant it. It didn't pay well. I was making around $32,000 a year, even with a master's degree. I knew I was just getting started. And this was a small company.

I learned what a blessing in disguise it was to work for a small company. There, I did anything and everything—duties I could never have done at a large company. When you do everything, you learn everything.

Another bonus was the company rule that anyone who worked past five p.m. was allowed to have a beer from the company fridge. I really had no complaints, especially when I stayed until 5:01.

It's Not How Much Money You Make but How Much You Keep That Makes You Wealthy

During my time at Jeff's company, Jeff drove us in his car to customer site visits. I think he was embarrassed by my car. He would always joke, "Don't I pay you enough? Can't you buy a new car?"

He wasn't wrong. My car was almost worthless. I'd gotten it for free! I stumbled across it while doing my internship. Before that, to get to the office, I rode two Greyhound buses, then walked a mile and a half. This was in 2001, and 9/11 had just happened. It was not an easy time to be a person with brown skin on public transportation in the US.

Then, out of the blue, my old roommate called and asked, "Do you want a car?" (That's right! We kept in touch.)

I replied, "Of course I want a car. I would love a car, but I can't afford to buy one!" A friend of his girlfriend had just gotten a new job and a new car. She wanted to get rid of her *very* old car. I called her, and she told me the car was rusty, and it hadn't been driven for about six months. I didn't care. I was just so thankful to have something. I took it to the mechanic and said, "Do what you have to do to get it to run, but know that I have no money." One hundred fifty dollars later, the car was running. I was now the proud owner of a rusty Toyota Corolla.

On those car rides with Jeff, we would sit and listen to sports. One time, I made a comment about how much money NFL players made. Jeff told me, "Remember, it's not how much money you make that makes you rich. Athletes file bankruptcy all time." I didn't know what he meant. I thought, *How does someone possibly go bankrupt with all that money?*

Jeff explained that it's not about the amount of money you make but what you do with it that matters. *That* is what determines how rich you will be. And that was the moment that prompted my interest in finance.

I began reading up on it, and I started investing shortly after. The company I worked for offered a 401k plan with a 3 percent match. But I was scared. I didn't want to *lose*. Well, that was a stupid mistake. I realized that inflation would outrun whatever money I saved. My money was better off in the market where it could grow tax-free. (This is why everybody needs financial education, especially young people.)

Everybody who works makes some money. Almost everybody wants to be rich. But most regular people aren't taught how to handle their money. Not even the basics. I started investing in my thirties, but I wish I had known to start sooner.

So that's my advice to you. Start saving and start investing.

A Risk Worth Taking

After working with Jeff at his company for a while, I was presented with an opportunity to work for a global company. Jeff's company was a small start-up, and I felt like I'd learned all I could there. So I left and began working for this new company. There, I stayed for several years, and although I was continuing to learn, I got the sense I should be doing *more*, that I wasn't tapping into my full potential. I wanted to have a bigger influence in the strategic decision-making at the company—I wanted to have a bigger impact on how efficiently the business was run, the direction it was going and the products we were releasing—and I just wasn't doing that.

Eventually, I applied for a position in San Diego, California, and got it. When I traveled there for the interview, I fell in love with the weather and the city, really all of California. It was just *wow*. This position was in the healthcare industry. I'd parted ways with it for my last job, and this felt like a reunion of sorts. My father being a doctor, health care was in my blood. While I never wanted to be a doctor, I always gravitated toward health care, just from a different perspective. Instead of engaging in check-ups, medicines, and surgeries, I'd be developing the technology to help others.

In San Diego, I became the leader of a program, which was a big deal for me. I'd never been an executive before. And now, I had *global* teams to manage. I was new; I was young, but I felt I brought a different perspective to the team. And we were a large team, so there, I had my initiation into corporate America.

There is definitely a *corporate* culture in the US, but I didn't know it. I was always polite, but at the same time, I didn't shy away like a few others tended to do. I always shared what I thought or felt. I learned how to tailor my message and its tone, depending on who I was speaking with, which turned out to have maximum impact. I compare it to playing on a sports team; you have to know how to talk to people and how to motivate your teammates. To inspire some, yelling works; for others, cursing does the job, and for others still, a soft message or gesture is required. The goal is to get them riled up and ready to play, and play to win. I was able to apply this technique to my career.

In addition to tailoring my communication skills, I could explain complicated technical ideas in simple terms to the leadership of the company so they could understand it in layman's terms. That's not always easy. The tech department is always filled with geeks, and the business world doesn't understand them. But if leadership had a tough question, they would call me, often bypassing several layers of leadership. They saw me as capable and eager. Being able to both *do* and *communicate* is a huge skill. It is a career skill everybody should develop but especially people in technology.

It wasn't long before I got noticed at this company. My skills allowed me to get in front of the right people. Then, in 2011, I received the biggest opportunity of my life—a job to set up and run a research and development center outside of the US. This was a long way from where I began my career as a software engineer and project leader for a tiny company.

Part 3: THE BIG LEAP TO SUCCESS

The Importance of Preparing

To win the role, I was asked to make a thirty-minute presentation to the board of directors of the publicly traded company. I had never presented to a group like this, and I was visibly shaking. My direct leaders opened with an introduction; then, for the first time, I was in charge of the *actual* presentation to the board. These are the moments that make you grow up. I was up the night before, sweating and trying to figure out how to do this. But in the darkness of night, I learned how to prepare.

I had to explain the building I would choose, the talent pool I was looking at, and the overall plan I had, and I had to be ready for the range of questions they could ask me. I had seen my superiors answer questions before, and I'd noted how, as leaders, they responded. *Be quick on your feet; be smart*, I told myself.

I did my best to make a case for why we should do what I proposed and outlined my created plan for how we would do it. I ended up doing well enough to give them all the confidence they needed in me, and the project was given a green light.

They told me, "If you take the job and do well, you can come back. If it doesn't go well, then things may get hard." In other words, I may not have a role to come back to. Did I even *want* to do (risk) something like this? I had never done anything like this before in my career. I had a nice job and was making good money. Life was fine. And that level of comfort left me wondering, *What if it isn't successful?*

But here's the thing: people miss out by playing it too safe. You don't want to gamble, but you also don't want to limit yourself. Knowing the difference and recognizing when you have an opportunity is a learned skill. The fear of failure stops a lot of people from following their passions. This is counterintuitive, and if you give in to the fear, you'll only handicap yourself. You'll never achieve anything worth achieving if you hold yourself back.

My parents were always risk averse. They would never overstretch themselves. But I was different, willing to review situations and take the plunge if it felt right. The trick is, once you do take the risk, you can't start thinking about failure. It's like a team walking into a game and thinking they don't want to lose. Guess what will happen? They will lose. You have to go in not worrying about the result. Go in with drive, hunger, and willingness. When you go in this way, you have no other option but to stay focused.

This project and new role would prove a big challenge. The more I thought about it, the more I determined it was worth trying. I didn't want to regret anything, so I reminded myself that all regret is, is simply not doing something.

I shook their hands, and the company gave me the new title of general manager, handed me a plane ticket, and I was off.

Flying Business Class

I was surprised when I looked at the ticket to see I was flying business class; I had always flown economy. It was a huge deal to me. It was a fifteen-hour flight, and the seat would recline all the way back so I could lie flat instead of sitting in my chair. Also, there were fewer people, so the service was a lot better and the flight attendants had less to do and more patience. I thought, *This is amazing. This is the way to fly!* Once I landed, I took a taxi to the main office.

Step one was to find office space. I had zero experience with this. In order to choose the right location, I asked myself the following questions: 1) Where is the talent located? 2) Where are the universities located? I needed a place where I'd have access to good talent. I also wanted to create a space that would attract the right talent to come and work for me.

Once I settled on the location, I had to build the office space. The country head (head of the company for the country) was busy doing other things, so he asked a real estate agent to show me two buildings. Immediately, I knew these places weren't right for the project. The locations wouldn't work because the talent we needed was elsewhere. I told the agent the reason I needed to see other locations. He was hesitant because he didn't want to get in trouble. We went anyway.

I finally found a location I liked, but there was one problem: the building was family-owned. "I don't think they're going to give it to you," the realtor said. I asked for a meeting with the trustee anyway, to explain what our company did and how we helped people. I didn't try to sell him. He liked that I was genuine, and twenty minutes into the meeting, we shook hands. I'd not only negotiated my first commercial lease, but I'd come in way under what the real estate agent had estimated would be the rent.

I was excited to share the good news, but the head of the country pushed back on my decision. He brushed me aside a little bit because he'd had his heart set on the first location, which he'd arranged for me to see. It was a very nice office but because of the location, it would not have attracted the type of talent we needed. When I returned to the US, I explained the situation to my leadership. They asked plenty of questions, but in the end, they supported me, saying, "Okay, this is your job. We will go with your decision."

When I returned, the country president and I didn't have the best relationship; we were butting heads, but I persevered and continued to be polite and respectful to him.

I now had approval for the office space in the location I desired, and I was managing internal relationships as best I could while getting ready to dig in and build the office I envisioned.

Digging In

Now that I had settled on a building, step two was to furnish and design the office and to stay within a certain budget. It was a large empty floor with nothing in it, so I was starting with a blank canvas. Again, I had never done anything like this, so I knew I needed help. I called a few design companies and had them take me to offices they'd designed and built to get an idea of their work. These offices included a bank, a technology company, an automobile manufacturer, and a real-estate office.

Seeing each of these locations helped me understand what they meant when they used certain terms in the proposal that I was unfamiliar with. I could see how they'd utilize different spaces, and this was an education for me. I selected the best furniture from the places I'd seen and made a plan that could work for us. While designing, I focused on what I felt were the most important factors.

Light was extremely important. On the contractor's initial proposal, offices were placed around the outside of the space next to the windows and the employees' cubicles were placed in the center. I said, "I think I want to change this. Let's make it brighter. I want to create a more open space with more sunlight coming in. Let's put the offices in the center and the employees on the outside." This created more natural light and a more attractive place for people to come. I was nervous about it, though, because I'd not done anything like it before. Furthermore, I needed to stay within my budget. I didn't want to go back, asking for more money. And I didn't want to build something so outlandish that it looked great but wasn't usable. It had to make sense and cater to the values of the company, the employees, and the leadership. If I messed it up, I knew people would visit and say, "What the heck is going on here?"

Beyond the layout, there was the issue of office furniture. I remember the proposal illustrated a big conference room with fancy chairs and then very simple chairs for everyone else. The contrast of the cubicles, desks, and chairs for the employees versus those in the conference room was significant. It was like walking from a two-star into a five-star hotel, and it just didn't make sense to me. So I asked the consulting firm to bring me chairs to try out for the employees. It turns out the hardest thing to shop for is office chairs; there are over two hundred types! I asked them to bring me only ten different office chairs because I wanted to try them before I made my decision. For two weeks, my little office was full of chairs, and I would sit on one for an hour or so to try it and decide if it was comfortable enough—after which time I'd choose another and repeat the process.

I chose the nicest, most expensive chairs. I knew employees would be sitting in these chairs for eight hours a day, doing the majority of their work in them, and I wanted people to enjoy sitting at their desks. We put the cheap chairs in the conference room because those chairs should only be used for short meetings. It was doubly effective because we wanted staff to have short meetings, anyway—to address their topics and then get on with their work. Even though I'd never done anything like this before, this naturally felt more sensible.

Next, they showed me all the different materials and options for desks and cubicles. I chose the nicest materials for the desks, and I chose easy access points for the power outlets. I wanted the employees to have an enjoyable experience. All of this added up in the spend column, so I had to make cuts elsewhere.

Once the building was designed, it looked incredible. As a bonus, I came in one million dollars under budget! When the leadership of the company came to visit, they were amazed by both.

The next step was hiring. In my presentation, I estimated we'd hire thirty people in the first two years. We ended up hiring one hundred thirty in two and a half years, and the operation was beyond successful.

As I mentioned, initially, there was some conflict with the country's company president. We had different views and didn't see eye to eye, butting heads a lot. Perhaps he was still annoyed about the decision to go with the new office location and didn't believe it would be successful. I was also operating in his territory and had to work closely with him because I would need help from his team, and the corporate functions fell in his group.

We had come in under budget on the build-out, and within three and a half years, this office had become a flagship office and a showcase for people visiting. The company brought everyone to the office to see it. Even though the country president and I started off on the wrong foot, my consistent courtesy and respect toward him, as well as the success of our office, led to us having a great relationship. He became a huge advocate for me and wrote a glowing recommendation for me when I transitioned out of this role. The staff were, at the same time, happy to be part of the success and sad to see me go. They gave me a book with all their thoughts, and it was very moving and surreal. I felt overwhelmed and wasn't sure how to react. We'd done a lot of good work and had made a positive impact on the local economy. It was a major success—something I'm incredibly proud of to this day.

I knew from that moment that I accepted the opportunity to build and run the overseas office that the majority of the project was not going to be easy. That opportunity changed my work life forever. I had taken on a huge assignment and had done well—hitting it out of the park, as they say. The risk was enormous, but it paid off big too. In the beginning, I had no idea what I was doing, but it turned out that I had *the skills* to do it. I was pretty good at it too.

Everyone probably has skills they aren't aware of. Being open to opportunity is the only way anyone finds out what those skills are. And taking risks is usually required.

Take Bigger Risks Earlier in Life

Taking the general manager role was a pivotal moment. My choices at the time were to take it and risk failing or stay on the normal career path as an engineer within the company. It was a risk worth taking, and it turned out, I had the ingredients to succeed. I stepped out of my comfort zone and learned on the job. Sometimes people shy away from being uncomfortable, preferring to play in a safe space.

Coming to the US was a bigger decision than even this, but it felt as if I didn't have too many options back then, so it felt easier; I didn't have as much to lose. The second time I took a massive risk was when I accepted this general manager role. I was already a successful engineer with the company, and I had a comfortable life, which made it a lot harder to take the big risk. I had more to lose. In the end, it turned out pretty well.

Don't always play it safe, especially when you're young. If you take risks early on in life, then you have more cushion if you fail—you have the time to get back up. When you're older, with a spouse and maybe kids, it's harder to take risks because the impacts will not just be felt by you. Only you can determine if the risk is worth it but don't forget to think about what you might gain. Don't just focus on what you might lose.

After my three and half years in that overseas role, I started to think about coming back to the United States. I would be saying *goodbye* to something that I could've done for a lot longer. And I was making *a lot* of money. My company paid for my house and my kids' school (yes, I had gotten married), and even gave me a hardship allowance. I was pocketing almost all the money I made.

But I had to remember something: I took on this role because it was exciting. There were few opportunities like that, and I knew I would regret not doing it. The success I had enjoyed had become my legacy, and it had passed every expectation I'd had for it. However, I felt I had learned all I needed to through this experience, and I was ready for the next big adventure. I didn't want to get too comfortable, rather I wanted to continue to challenge myself and continue to build on all the new knowledge I had gained.

At the end of my assignment, on the plane back to the US, it sunk in for the first time—all the lives I'd touched, the number of people who had good things to say about me, and all of my experiences that had led me to this point. I felt I'd really made it. I'd done something good. That office is still running, and once in a while, somebody will send me a message. I received one the other day that said, "Your baby is still alive." And I feel proud of that.

But I had done everything I could, and I believed, once again in my career, there was nothing left to learn there. I had done my time, built a team, and imparted cultural values. Essentially, I had built an extension of my company and developed a system that would be followed for years to come. I had learned the skills, and I believed the next challenge was to apply those skills to something bigger. Plus, I always harbored the desire to return to America, so back I went.

Coming Home

I arrived back in the US to a new role in the same company. Eventually, the company got bought over by an even larger company. Nevertheless, life was good. Everything was good.

I had changed, though. I had done the hard work and had succeeded. That hard work that translated into success brought me more confidence. I had learned so much, and it showed. It showed in my conversations with important people, through my lack of hesitancy, and in my ability to come up with new ideas. I stood out in a good way. That type of confidence is hard to fake, and it only comes from layering successes, including the success that comes by way of risk. Nothing can compensate for those real-life experiences.

I had the best boss. He pulled some strings so that I could join his team. The only way I can describe him is a *guy's guy*. We would go out for a beer together and relax, leaving work at the office. He was charming and sophisticated when he needed to be—when the time was right. He gave me complete freedom, so there was no micromanaging, no questioning of my choices, but full trust. It was really wonderful.

Around this time, another company reached out to me about a new position they had. This company was an up-and-coming organization in the US. Essentially, this would be an opportunity to create a strategy for the company's roadmap in the US market. It would be an opportunity to *drive* the product strategy. I told them I wasn't interested, though. I was content where I was, with my good job and a good boss, and I was enjoying the company culture and vision.

However, there was something I was missing: being a part of something *smaller*. Remember, this company had been bought by a massive organization. This changed things so that, unless the product you were working on was worth hundreds of millions of dollars, you were not being seen by the executives—the real decision-makers. I felt I lacked the ability to really make an impact on the organization and on the lives of clinicians and patients. I had become just another cog in the wheel of the organization.

So I reconsidered the new opportunity with which I'd been presented. With this new organization, I'd have a greater ability to make a difference. They had good products and a smaller market share. If I took this new job, I knew I would have the chance to take this company from a newcomer to a major player in the US market. I wanted the challenge to drive change. So I opted to interview for the role.

My first interview went well. We had a pleasant conversation, but I still wasn't sold. After a few weeks, I still hadn't heard back from them, so I thought they'd dismissed me. Maybe it wasn't meant to be. About a month later, I was surprised to hear from them. The head of HR reached out and asked, "Are you still interested?"

I agreed to a second interview. This time, I was being interviewed by the grandson of the company's founder. This was the interview that sealed the deal for me. This global CEO was so different from the typical CEOs I'd come across in the US. He was humble, hardworking, and even nice. During the interview, he stressed getting to know me as *a person*. He wanted to know what my passions were, what motivated me. I appreciated that.

I was happy to hear they appreciated me too; they made an offer, which I accepted. My new job title was CTO (chief technology officer). It was time to leave my current employer. I had spent ten years with this company, and it was hard to say goodbye, but I handed in my notice, knowing it was the right decision for my family and for me. Even though my boss tried hard to get me to stay, he was gracious enough to let me go with his best wishes for my future. I knew opportunities like this new one were rare and believed it was another risk worth taking.

Building Trust

My new job started off rough. From my first day, I could sense the immense distrust within different teams, and I knew this was going to be an issue. In my last position, creating an R&D center from scratch, I had a clean slate; everything was new, including the employees, which meant no one came with preconceived notions, and it was easier to train people. However, this time was different. Here, I had an existing set of players with their own set of issues. There was a mix of relationships—some good, others bad. I needed to instill change, and I discovered quickly that creating strategies and products is much simpler than changing an established culture.

Once I accepted this fact, I thought, *All right, let's get to work.* I understood the business already, so I focused on two key actions: building relationships and gaining trust. It was a huge task to turn the culture around. It takes a lot of time for people to develop trust with one another when it's already been broken. They have to see that you mean what you say and say what you mean. I needed a team full of people who were willing to share what was on their minds, and I needed to surround myself with right-minded people so that the right things could happen.

Slowly, we turned around the culture, which had a positive impact on the business as a whole. Employee satisfaction rose; efficiency increased, as did sales. It didn't happen overnight—it took about twenty-four months. I knew there was a valuable lesson for me here too. And that was you can do almost anything if you're motivated, genuine, and willing to accept constructive criticism. Still today, I believe making that cultural change was my biggest accomplishment in business—even more so than starting an office from scratch in another country.

When I achieve a goal, I sometimes forget to celebrate. I assume that because it's over, I should immediately jump into the next project. When I slow down and make time to reflect, the process always seems more beautiful to me than the result. I look back at growing up in India, being in college, studying, being around friends, and meeting many talented people, and always remember the challenging times fondly because those times forced me to grow. They forced me to learn, change, adapt, and become a better version of myself. Perhaps because the growth process is the best part of the journey, I enjoy every part of the journey, not just the destination.

Becoming CEO

In July 2018, I was traveling internationally when I got to know that I was being offered the position of CEO. Instead of going out and celebrating with the rest of the group, I walked back to my hotel alone. That's when it hit me. *Holy shit—what just happened?* It was surreal that I'd made it to this point in my career. It was bizarre thinking I will be a *CEO*.

I thought about how I'd grown up. I thought about my grandfather's words and how true they were. "Low aim is a crime. Know that you can achieve whatever you want in life." Those words allowed me to be bold enough to risk failing, and I'm glad I accepted the opportunity to be courageous. I knew I had talent, but I had no idea what to do with it. I learned I had what it takes: the self-belief, the resilience, the courage, and the trust . . . that if I took the next right step, events would unfold in my favor. If I put my mind to it, I knew I could perform well. Anybody else who is hungry enough can do it too—if they're willing to put in the effort.

I'm not disillusioned. I know my life is an example of grabbing opportunities that come at the right time. But because of the hard work I put forth and the confidence I had, I was better prepared for both the lucky breaks and the earned opportunities that came my way. I didn't squander them.

Here's my message to you: If you're young, start. Don't be afraid. Take the leap. Challenge yourself, and don't settle. Aim to achieve something outside of your grasp. Do not be limited by what you *think* is possible. Too many people hesitate for too long. I believe the human brain is the most powerful thing to ever exist, and we underestimate it and its true power. God has made us capable, indeed. If you aim to grasp what feels just out of reach, if you take that leap of faith, the path will appear. Just begin.

This is your road trip—you get to plan the route, map out the sites to see, and visualize the destination. What are you waiting for?

Conclusion

I've had a lot of failures, especially early in my life. I wasn't the most popular kid or the brightest or the smartest. My attempts at playing sports didn't work out too well; however, the skills I learned while playing team sports helped me professionally. I learned to spot the right talent, build excellent teams, and motivate those teams toward success. Everyone is different, so one message doesn't work for everyone. I had to figure out how to adapt my communication, depending on who I was speaking with to get the best out of people.

Throughout my early thirties, I just kept trying. I tried a lot of things, and I failed a lot. But I enjoyed the process of growing, building, trying, and eventually doing things to their completion, rather than only enjoying the end results. I learned a lot from my failures, and that's the trick; I didn't give up. I turned them into opportunities to further my education. I'm glad I tried a lot of different things. I'd like to impart this wisdom: "Never give up on your dreams."

Because I followed this advice myself, I've been able to achieve a lot. An accomplishment I'm proud of that I haven't mentioned yet is that a few years back, John Hopkins University, one of the leading universities in the world, invited me to give a talk at their School of Medicine. I was terribly honored to be invited, and it was one of my proudest moments. My parents would have been thrilled if they'd been able to see me.

I was thrilled too.

About the Author

Harsh Dharwad is an experienced global leader who is passionate about solving healthcare challenges with technological solutions that make a difference in the lives of patients and clinicians. He excels at simplifying complex problems, building high-performing cultures, and empowering teams to execute the vision of an organization.

He enjoys mentoring new graduates and entrepreneurs with their start-ups and guiding new talent to achieve their full potential.

Harsh is involved in regular speaking engagements where he provides thought leadership and mentorship to entrepreneurs, healthcare professionals and students.

For any enquiries please contact –

book.gochaseit@gmail.com

www.ingramcontent.com/pod-product-compliance
Lightning Source LLC
Chambersburg PA
CBHW070157230526
45471CB00002B/706